This book wouldn't have been possible without the help of many people. To my editor Carolyn Messere, your gifted hands of moulded my madness into a work of art.   To AJ Leon, thanks for allowing me to test these ideas on stage at the inaugural Misfit Conference. Kamal Ravikant and James Altucher you've taught me how to find my voice, to bleed on the page, and to leave my heart on stage.   Mars Dorian, you're the definition of unmistakable which is why you were the the most obvious cover artist for this book. To Greg Hartle, thanks for being a friend, advisor, and teaching me to see opportunity in adversity. To my parents, thank you for providing a shelter and a space in which I get to create Art. To the Small Army of people who have listened to BlogcastFM and tolerated my ridiculously long Facebook status updates, this book is for you. I hope it guides you on your own path to being unmistakable.

I always enjoy hearing from the people who read my books. You can follow me on twitter @skooloflife or send me an email to srini@blogcastfm.com

TABLE OF CONTENTS

FOREWORD

The future belongs to the misfits.

Perhaps it always has.

It seems fitting that I'm writing this at Burning Man, a strange and alternative pop-up city that had to venture into the middle of nowhere – an ancient lakebed in the Nevada desert, known as the playa – to bring itself into being near the end of every August.

Each time I come here, to this world of portapotties, alkaline dust storms, sweltering days, freezing nights, and no Starbucks – I swear to myself, this is the last freaking time. And yet there's a point when something in me shifts over and I know I will return. How could I not? "Welcome home," Burners say as we reunite with each other on the playa, and it's true. Even if you've never been here before, the playa calls you home.

This is where your inner misfit can come out to play.

This morning, walking to Center Camp, I watched a guy ride around in an art car built to resemble a giant roast chicken. I like to imagine him waking up one morning (in his ordinary life, in the ordinary world) brushing his teeth, checking the weather and the traffic report, bracing himself for another day at his

San Francisco startup, and realizing: *I must build an art car that resembles a giant roast chicken.*

It wouldn't have been his carefully polished, expensively educated, khaki-pants-and-buttondown persona that decided this. He probably didn't see it as a way to get women into bed ("Hi. I'm building a giant chicken. Want to have sex?") His colleagues at work, his drinking buddies, his best friend, the cute but shy waitress at his favorite diner who has been crushing on him for six months, probably never looked at him and thought, *Within that man there lurks a giant-roast-chicken-rider, bursting to be unleashed upon the world.*

But he knew there was something deep inside him, weird and whimsical and apart from the structures of everyday life, that needed to play. It might not have made sense in any "rational" way, but not everything does, or is meant to; it just is what it is, and what it must be.

It's your inner misfit.

This is all very well, you might be thinking to yourself, *and maybe even slightly amusing, but what the hell do tales of roast-chicken-riders have to do with my plans to dominate the world?*

Earlier today a thirtysomething entrepreneur (decked out in Mad Max gear) was in my RV, telling me about his business, which has something to do with shipping readymade bags of supplies to people about to climb Mount Everest. Soon, he told me, all the delivery trucks will be automated; they will glide to your door, text your cell to announce their arrival, discharge packages at your feet. This elimination of the human will cut costs for many and increase profits for a few – and put two to three million people out of work.

What he didn't say – and didn't need to – was how the same story will play itself out across industries.

In his book A WHOLE NEW MIND, Daniel Pink describes how the forces of automation, outsourcing, and an overabundance of products are ushering in a new era. Call it the Conceptual Age, or the Creative Age. The important thing, Pink writes, is that if you want to survive (much less thrive) you need to ask yourself three questions about whatever it is that you do:

Can a computer do it for you?
Can someone overseas do it cheaper?
Is what I'm offering in demand in an age of abundance?

The only job security, to the extent that it exists, will reside in your ability to be "high concept high touch": to come up with inspired and innovative ideas, gain creative insights, and connect with people on an emotional level through empathy, story or design. To do what computers can't, or that dude in China or India for only so many dollars an hour. To create experiences that people didn't know they wanted or needed but soon refuse to live without.

To turn your work – and perhaps life itself – into art, in a way that is unique to you and relevant to others.

It probably won't look like a giant roast chicken. Burning Man is not the so-called real world. But the real world is changing faster and faster, and the same creativity that's been pushed to the edges – that seemed to belong only to artists in some mysterious Bohemia, or individuals in strange careers requiring them to wear black turtlenecks – must now find its way into everyday life.

I'm reminded of Albert Einstein's quote: "No **problem** can be **solved** from the same level of consciousness that created it."

When you look at the problems that threaten not just our livelihood as individuals but our future as a species, it's pretty clear that we need a new consciousness.

We need new voices, new stories, new solutions, new truths…to revise the old ones and replace the broken ones, to lead us through this shifting, quicksand present and create a future that doesn't end up a repeat of the past but is truly *created*.

One day at a time.

One individual at a time.

You start to do this by tuning in to the still small voice that lives within us all, and allowing it to guide your choices and decisions.

I think of this voice as a soul-voice: the deep, coded line of poetry that is the essence of you, pushing to find expression in the world. The more successful we are at manifesting it, the more authentic we consider our lives to be. Instead of living out a secondhand narrative, we create a fresh one of our own.

We can't just *tell* our truth.

We have to *live* it. We have to *embody* it.

Creativity, then, is more than just a modern business advantage. It is a state of mind and a way of life. It also doesn't leave us any hiding places. We are what we make. Our creations show the truth of who we are. They also shape how -- or if -- the world remembers us when we're gone.

This is the sacred dance. It demands nothing less than everything you've got to give it. Creativity builds on itself, and so does creative living. As Srini notes, things have a way of revealing themselves only once you're in pursuit of them. This generally means that you have to start running on faith.

Most people are afraid.

Most people get comfortable in a life that seems tolerable enough. They don't have the time, they complain, and may actually believe it (even as they spend hours watching TV, playing video games, surfing the Internet, at the mall). The price is that moment near the end when you realize that your life never belonged to you.

You never stepped up. You never owned it.

You never showed us who you really are.

And I started to wonder, Srini writes, *what would happen if we left our heart on stage every time we created anything.*

It's a bust your ass to shine, honest to a fault, no

bullshit, zero apology performance. If you look at the work of some of the most successful people in the world you'll see it as the undertone. It isn't just something they do, it's who they are. It's the kind of performance where your heart and soul bleed.

I like that a lot.

We learn early and repeatedly that we can be hurt. We figure out ways, growing up, to shelter and protect our inner misfit. Our tender vulnerable soul-voice.

Our task, now, is to destroy all those old structures, out in the world and deep within us. To shrug off the armor, strip away the bullshit, open ourselves up and out with the tenderness and vulnerability of the child we no longer are – so we can take our power as adults and build a new kind of life, an authentic life, that sets our inner misfits to play in a world that doesn't yet realize how badly it needs them.

Somewhere between what your soul knows and what the world wants you to know, is your choice about what kind of story you will live and how you will live it.

Our inner misfits are wiser than we are, and whispering to us all the time.

The only question is: are we listening?

Justine Musk
Black Rock City, Nevada

Introduction

All this started with a couple of questions on my birthday. What if 34 had been the last year of my life? Would I have been happy with how I had lived it? The answer was a resounding NO. But I think Patti Digh has a much more eloquent way of putting this. She says I have to eliminate the false dichotomy between my current life and the end of my life.

There are plenty of things I had thought would have already happened by this point in my life. If I had told the 20-year old ego-driven version of myself how things got derailed, he might think I'd lost my mind. He would wonder how I screwed up all his grand plans of $100 dinners, fancy cars and being referred to as Mr. Rao. I'm sure he'd be thrilled if I said,

"Dude, I traded in any shot you had at the board room for a pair of board shorts."

But it's only through experience that you gain wisdom and knowledge. These are just some of my observations of a life that hasn't gone according to plan.

I've been fired more than a handful of times. More about that later. A guy at a BIG market research company told me I wasn't the type of person who was interested in controlling my destiny. Last I checked, he was still working there.

On every birthday you come a year closer to dying. It

sounds cliche but life is short. That's why I'm embracing YES. My friend Kamal Ravikant says, "You just say yes and life molds itself around you." So yes to rock concerts, flying lessons, surf trips, chocolate cake, and great sex (or whatever your version is of those things).

Become unmistakable

Nothing matters. That's the key to unlocking the handcuffs that keep us imprisoned in worry, self-doubt, fear and disbelief. I've never gained anything from excessive concern about what matters in my life. When we're excessively concerned, we attach ourselves to outcomes, most of which are out of our control. As a result, our sense of who we are fluctuates based on the outcomes in our lives. None of these things define you as a person:

Your education
The size of your bank account
Your job title
Your failures
Your successes

And sadly, we let so many of these things rule our lives. Obsession with crossing off the checkboxes of society's life plan leads to little other than therapy, midlife crises, and depression.

What if we just ditched all the checkboxes?

What if there were no rules?

What if we wrote our own rules?

What if we approached our life like a work of art? Rich and colorful with stories, scenic backdrops, and soundtracks that make us sing with delight.

What if we learned to be TRULY present and realize that this moment right now is the only one that's guaranteed.

What if AJ Leon's wise words that "this is not your practice life" became the filter for all your decisions? How would that change the decisions you make?

How much happier could we possibly be?

Become the No-Bullshit Version of You

What would happen if you were truly honest with yourself and the world around you?

What would happen if you actually said what you were thinking -- honest, imperfect, unedited, and unfiltered?

What would happen if you decided to be the no-bullshit version of yourself?

- The one that's not afraid to take risks
- The one that's not afraid to tell the truth
- The one that isn't concerned with validation
- The one that creates for the joy of creating, nothing more

What would happen if you let your inner child be in charge for a while and let your outer adult sit on the bench? Imagine the beauty that would fill our world when people stop wasting their unique gifts on the pursuit of becoming somebody else.

What would happen if we pursued being unmistakable instead of wildly successful by external measures?

Chances are you would piss some people off. However, you would also find the people who love you, look forward to hearing from you and miss you when you are gone. This is the purest possible place you can create anything from, and yet fear and ego keep us from doing this. Instead, we play in a space of ego-based creation. We work on increasing open rates, page views, and followers instead of the impact that we could have. The counterintuitive nature of this is that if you work on impact, the other things take care of themselves.

Everybody has a microphone. Do not use it to create

sheep, clones, and copies of yourself. Use it to help people discover their unique gifts. The louder your microphone (i.e. the bigger your audience), the greater your responsibility is for this. In addition, remember that there is no competition for a "No bullshit" version of who you are.

Become REALLY good at something

Most jobs teach us to be average at a bunch of things, and when we fall below average at those things, we work on fixing our weaknesses through performance improvement plans, and a bunch of other bullshit that causes us to remain mediocre. Instead, become a specialist at something. My friend James Altucher says that reinvention is a 5 year process. It can also change your life. I haven't been struggling. I've been reinventing myself over the last few years.

We've entered what James refers to as the "choose yourself" era. You can publish your own book, record your own album, or curate your own museum. So go out and do it. Choose yourself. Middlemen are kind of a dying breed and who wants to do things their way? My friend AJ Leon returned his advance to the publisher because the book he was going to write was going to be terrible. Instead he did everything his way.

Become an Inextinguishable Blaze

I think there's a fire burning in every one of us to make a dent in the universe. But, it gets extinguished by the mediocre visions of those who defend the status quo encouraging us to be practical and realistic. I tried doing it that way for many years.

I did what was practical.

I made every decision based on its external value.

- How good would it look on paper?

- How much would it pay?

- What would it be worth down the road?

- Who could I impress with these accolades?

- Would this put me on that path to being "Big swinging DI#$#k" ? (Watch Wall Street if you don't get the reference).

And eventually the fire went out. I went numb and I didn't even know it. When you're that numb, you can't even feel it when the fire burns out.

You just sleepwalk.

You say yes to things you should say no to.

You use external solutions to solve internal problems. Excessive spending, alcohol and closets full of shit you don't need keep you doing work you hate, so you can maintain this vicious cycle.

Vices seem like your only true joy.

Comparison keeps you trapped in a competition of trying to win at the game of society's life plan.

Then suddenly, you realize there are no winners, no losers. Jaclyn Mullen had a beautiful way of looking at this when she commented on Facebook on the loss of the Spurs:

"Sometimes you win, sometimes you lose! But all you can do is play the game of life second by second, minute by minute...play by play. There's a lot to learn from this NBA Finals! You fight to the finish, you give everything you've got with every ounce of determination and heart you have. I'm happy the Heat won but I'm even happier at the resiliency the Spurs have demonstrated. And in the end if you think about it, San Antonio didn't lose a thing :) Both teams are true champions!"

That's when the spark gets lit, and the real fire begins.

You play for your love of the game.

You create because creation is its own reward.

Joy bleeds through everything you touch, and your desire to make a dent in the universe becomes an inextinguishable blaze that will ignite anybody who comes in contact with you.

THE FUTURE OF WORK

Put your signature on everything you do. It will lead you to some unexpected and amazing places.

The idea of a job for life is a complete myth. The whole concept of a career path is being dismantled before our eyes. Standing out in a sea of resumes where people present bullshit versions of who they are to match up bullet points in job description is a fool's errand. It's a recipe for work you hate.

A friend who thought everything was smooth sailing after a rather strenuous job search found out he might be let go in two months. The industry he's working in had a major change.

After 13 months of playing at the top of my game at a job I loved, the project I was working on at a day job got tabled. A few months later I was let go.

Not long ago, one of my freelance writing gigs ended.

In the past, a loss like this would send me into a minor tailspin of lighting up a cigarette and drinking just enough to numb the pain.

But, I've realized that loss creates an opening in our lives. We can fill that space with fear, panic and anxiety. Or we can let it be open for creating something new, something that didn't exist before. It can lead to something far better. To experience something new, we have to let go of what's old. We have to remain calm in the face of setbacks.

Most people get trapped here. They get stuck on the

idea that their current circumstances are permanent. This dictates their choices, behavior, and worldview. As a result, they don't stretch themselves.

The point of a loss isn't to get back to where you were before the loss. It's the chance to replace what was there with something much better. It's an opportunity for reinvention, radical transformation and infinite possibility.

In the last few months, each time a loss occurred in my life, something SIGNIFICANTLY better has replaced it.

- More money from other sources

- Unexpected Opportunities

- The start of a New Chapter

The first time you get punched in the face, it's gut-wrenching. You might get knocked out. The second time, you might fall down on the mat. The third time, you get a black eye. Eventually you become desensitized and you barely even flinch. Once you get to this place, it's liberating. You can move on quickly and navigate the uncertain waters that are par for the course in any entrepreneurial journey.

Get on a skill path instead of a career path

When I got out of business school, I had a rude awakening. I had no real skills. I had mastered passing tests, collecting overpriced pieces of paper (aka degrees), and decorating walls with these so-called badges of honor. But I was a commodity. I didn't know how to actually do anything. I had miraculously survived an era where a degree and a resume were the ticket to a job. In the last few years, that's changed.

A few weeks ago, I spoke with Cal Newport, the author of *So Good They Can't Ignore You*. One of the things he said is that our future depends on our ability to develop rare and valuable skills.

Figure out what those are. Put your signature on everything you do. It will lead you to some unexpected and amazing places.

THE FIRST TIME I GOT FIRED

My greatest sin was to waste my life believing that I wasn't capable of something more.

It was December 20, 2001. I wasn't feeling well. I was never feeling well at that job. In the midst of it, I developed a case of irritable bowel syndrome. It was my first job out of college.

Here's a bit of advice. If you're building a startup and the team goes out to Indian food regularly, have more than one bathroom in your building. Otherwise one of your employees might get IBS.

I spent 9 months waking up at 5:30 am, commuting and coming home at 8 pm every single day. It was frowned upon to leave before 7. So I stayed until 7.

The CEO threatened all of us with the idea that there were no other jobs out there. He tried to motivate people with fear and a glimmer of hope. When you motivate people by fear they do just enough not to get fired. But it didn't make a difference.

-The software still didn't work.

- The culture was still terrible and everybody hated working there.

- A software engineer was asked to come back early from his wedding in India.

- Somebody got fired at least once a week.

You just wondered if you were next. We would have these company meetings where people would be introduced as new employees and you'd never see them again.

I was already showing signs of being a corporate misfit (I just hadn't completely embraced my inner misfit). I wasn't afraid to tell the CEO what I actually thought. Most people thought I was insane because he'd probably fire me. Amazingly enough he didn't (for a while).

I drank ALOT when I was at that job. On the weekends I numbed myself with excessive amounts of vodka and red bull and stayed out until the sun was almost rising. Now I wake up before the sun rises so I can surf (this is a much better lifestyle).

I went to work that Friday morning, 5 days before Christmas. Timing for firing somebody wasn't exactly our CEO's specialty. But at least I got a much longer vacation. We went to lunch to celebrate a friend's resignation. When we got back from lunch I was called into an office for an impromptu meeting. The VP of sales who had just started said, "Srini, we're going to have to let you go." I started crying. Looking back I should have been relieved. My friend who had the good-bye lunch celebration said I stole his thunder by getting fired.

You see, loss creates an opening in your life. But if you fill it with panic, anxiety, fear and all sorts of other bullshit, you can't create anything new in that space.

But I cried. I was devastated that I had pissed away such a significant chunk of my life on something so awful. This is why I value my time so much. This is why I trust my gut when I feel like an employment situation could be a disaster. I'm usually right.

I became desensitized to getting fired after this because this was the start of a 10 year journey that would eventually cause my life topple like a house of cards.

The First of Many Confessions of a Corporate Misfit:

My greatest sin was to waste my life believing that I wasn't capable of something more.

I had just finished grad school and was dabbling with my "100 Reasons You Should Hire Me" project. A few weeks later, I abandoned the project because I couldn't come up with 100 reasons for anybody to hire me. I don't even think I had 100 bullet points on my resume.

So I just started writing and The Skool of Life was born. I'd write for an hour, apply for jobs, and head to the beach to surf. I realized about a week after I graduated that sitting in front of the computer all day was a recipe for depression.

Eventually I ran completely out of money. A friend agreed to rent my apartment and let me sleep on the floor whenever I needed to. So I moved back to my parents' house, and every other week I was sleeping on the floor in a place that used to be mine. I got an allowance because I was so broke. It was ridiculous.

I stretched my $50 allowance for 5 days in LA.

- I took flasks to bars so I'd never have to buy drinks
- I'd email the organizers of events and work the door, so I got in free
- PB&J became a staple in my diet

And of course I surfed. That was the start of a lifelong journey.

Sometime in July of 2009, I found myself at the beach from Wednesday to Sunday. I surfed all day every day during those 5 days. That was the end of my life as I knew it. It turned out I had discovered the perfect hobby for an unemployed person. Surfing took a shitload of time and it didn't cost any money.

I got to the beach earlier every single day

I learned how to read the surf report

I learned that you got up early to avoid the wind

I started to bring a loaf of bread and PB&J. Once I left my duffel bag open, and a bunch of seagulls ate my bread. I didn't eat very well that day.

I scheduled job interviews around surf conditions. I did a phone interview from the beach. Another time I had to go to San Diego, so I scheduled the interview in the late afternoon. I spent the whole day surfing. I changed from board shorts into an actual suit in the parking lot. Believe me, I got some strange looks from other surfers. I had to tell them, "I'm going to a job interview." They forgave me for looking so buttoned up.

Every single time somebody saw me they would say, "Wow you've become really dark." I resisted the temptation to be a smart ass and say, "You've gained a lot of weight since I last saw you." But I was definitely getting tanned. Indian people don't typically sunburn (with some exceptions). We just get really dark.

A way to pass the time was quickly becoming a way of life. While my world felt like it was in shambles, the ocean was the ultimate escape. Every time I got out of the water I was happy. Nothing mattered as much as I thought it did. (Mostly it still doesn't).

It was the only place I felt truly at peace. It still is. I don't know how I ever lived without it. I think I would have probably died from misery if it hadn't been for the ocean. For a while people probably thought I slept under a lifeguard tower in Santa Monica. I remember some guy saying, "damn dude, you're always here." And I was.

Sometime in November I found a job. I quit in 2 weeks. The next morning I was back at the beach. Some people think surfing caused me to quit that job. I even heard through a friend that people thought surfing was ruining my life. In fact do a google search for surfing has ruined my life and you'll end up at my blog rather quickly. I figured this out when I was doing a search for a bumper sticker.

Dave Conrey asked me about the role that surfing has played in the work I do. I said, "It's everything. It's the foundation and the driving force of my life. It's the best thing that's ever happened to me." Thank God for that endless summer.

COMPASS VS MAP

Straight and narrow paths rarely lead to interesting destinations

In the first part of our life, we are given a compass. There is little structure to the way we're educated. We are given the freedom to determine our own direction. Kindergarten classrooms are utter chaos and true genius at the same time. The potential to discover a calling is available every single day. Then something happens. Somebody decides that you might stray too far off the beaten path, and gives you a map. They decide what is important for your future, and these decisions become the destinations on the map.

If I were to use a map long enough, eventually I would become fearful of ditching it for a compass.

However, if I want to do interesting work, take risks, and see what I am really made of, I have to be willing to use a compass instead of a map. The day I ditched the map for the compass is the day I walked of the edge of the Earth, and my work became an experience that only I can create for people. Every time I have been given a map, I have gotten lost. The map was based on where somebody else wanted me to end up. By following that map, at best I will become a pale imitation of the person who drew the map.

The thing with using a compass instead of a map is that I don't know the hurdles, the roadblocks, and potholes that might occur. However, on the unpaved path there is often scenic beauty along the way. Straight and narrow paths rarely lead to interesting destinations.

There's this myth perpetuated by social programming of "having it all figured out." That is complete bullshit. Nobody has it all figured out. If they did, why do so many people with a ton of money seem so completely depressed about their lives? Why is the person who has the picture perfect life (aka American Dream) so dissatisfied with the quality of his or her life? It is just proof that nobody ever has it all figured out. The thing is that we are perpetual students of the school of life. There are no grades, no graduation, just life-long learning.

In the early part of our life, when we use a compass, we are learning. However, when we use a map, it screws up everything.

- We start to memorize

- We shut off the possibility of interesting conclusions

- We rule out the potential of undiscovered destinations

We do this all because we want to arrive at the right answer or place we're supposed to.

If I had plans to climb a mountain and ended up at the beach, somebody might say I screwed up. I say, time to grab a surfboard, paddle out and catch a few good waves. It all depends on how I look at it. I know because I had plans to climb the ladder all the way into a corner office, and I literally ended up at the ocean. To paraphrase Seth Godin, maybe we should look for an interesting answer instead of the right one.

To become truly unmistakable I have to be willing to ditch the map, travel without a guidebook, and see where it leads me. It is an unscripted life, and that is a damn good thing because it means I get to write my own story. Be unafraid to occasionally stop and ask for directions (especially if I am running around in circles).

When I look at what my life would have become if I had ended up on that path, I am grateful for a life that hasn't gone according to plan. The plan was not even mine. I was given a map far too early in life.

Treat this guide as a compass. I can only point you in a direction. You must pave your own path.

Every single time you make a decision in your life, you go in a certain direction and you cut off the possibility of another one.

A few years ago I wrote down my list of goals and dreams. Then I filed them away and hoped they would magically happen. But they never did. That's because I treated them more as a wishlist than a prophecy.

So instead of a map, I wrote 500 words that describe my life in 2 years. This is my compass. It's the filter through which I make decisions and choices. I realized this morning that even my daily to-do list should be determined by this compass.

Of course, you should allow for spontaneity and be willing to explore the scenic route. After all, that's part of what life is about. And by now, I know that life rarely goes exactly according to plan. If you're open to the possibility, it will go far better than you ever thought it would.

There's a certain joy in uncertainty and the

unexpected experiences of our lives. The conversations you never planned on and the opportunities you didn't anticipate are always things you should consider. But letting those 500 words serve as a compass for your goals and dreams makes them much more likely to happen.

If making a decision throws you so far off course that you're facing the polar opposite direction of where you want to end up, it might be the wrong decision, since it practically guarantees you won't end up in the direction your compass is pointing you.

Let's say you want to be an artist of some sort and for the next 100 days you sit on your ass in front of the television. Well that's a completely different direction than the one your dream is pointing you in. But if you have the habit of sketching, drawing, doodling something every single day and correcting your course just a tiny bit during each step along the way, you'll eventually end up at your destination.

Too often I see people break out their compass and promptly go 180° from the direction of a dream. The sketch above is something I drew yesterday. It's only a partial list of the 500 word summary of how I described my life in 2 years. It's the compass for my choices. It's the filter through which I'll make most of my decisions...

And as I was reminded, "there's no surfing there." So I'm working on adding that.

A COMMITMENT TO YOUR CRAFT

People don't get good at things by working on them when they're inspired or feel like it. Some mornings I don't feel inspired to write. Everything sounds like it's coming out the wrong end. But these are the most important times to write. These are the times that separate the people who Steven Pressfield refers to as pros from the amateurs. But how long are you willing to act like a pro without any of the external rewards that come with it?

I would go so far as to say that you shouldn't put an expiration date on any dream that really matters to you. I'd love to fill your ear with stories of guts and glory. But sometimes it's just a grind of doing things that aren't all that exciting.

- You put the coffee back in the microwave because it gets cold

- You hack at little details because the edges matter so much

- You watch Youtube videos trying to figure out how to align margins that most people will never notice because of the one person that will notice.

- You watch your emotions like a Six Flags roller coaster, up and down, inside out, and upside down. Then you have a drink (depending on what time of day it is).

- You wonder about the day when none of this will be part of it, but that's a myth because every single day is about reinvention.

- You reinvent yourself, your words, your art,

or whatever dent you want to make in the universe.

And in the midst of the grind, there's little bits of excitement that you can't find in other work:

- An email from a stranger who was touched by something you said
- A friend who has a better day because you were a part of it
- And the occasional external accolade that feeds your ego

So now you're left with some questions.

- How far are you willing to go?
- How long will you stick with it?
- What if you know now there is no finish line?

Are you willing to make a commitment to a craft? There is no right or wrong answer. Just the answer that makes your heart sing and lights your eyes on fire.

MIMICRY AND REPLICA

"Why do I need a personal brand? Why should that be any different from the honest me? Are people afraid to show their real selves?"(rhetorical question because the obvious answer is "yes")." - James Altucher

If you try to mimic, copy, or emulate anybody else, at best you will be a pale imitation

Mimicry is not the point. The goal is not to create a replica of somebody else's life that you hope you will admire as much as you admire theirs. You might look at somebody like AJ Leon and think that is what you want to be.

However, you have your own remarkable misfit inside of you. It's based on your experiences, your stories, your WISDOM. Something tells me that **you** are who he would want you to be too.

If you try to mimic, copy, or emulate anybody else, at best you will be a pale imitation.

My friend Greg Hartle almost let best practices destroy his amazing story. I think he is out of his mind for walking out of his door with ten dollars and a laptop. But that's also why I love his story. It is his. I do not want to trade lives with him.

Mars Dorian has mastered the art of being unmistakable. You can look at something he has drawn and know it is his. The cover of this book was done by him. It is one of the most admirable goals to achieve.

Tell YOUR story. Tell it in a way that only you can.

Maybe my words today will serve as a guide. But don't treat them as gospel. Some people hate my work. I have been called a disservice to humanity (no exaggeration). Take what works for you; discard the rest.

Do not TRY to create. Create.

"What if you created a space for yourself where there are no mistakes, no failures, only lessons, and each lesson takes you closer to that place you don't know you're going but will recognize when you get there?"- Justine Musk

Your ego is the bullshit version of who you are, and ego-based creation is not your art

There is a creative space I am able to enter in which I get completely absorbed in what I am doing. The world around me disappears. The voices in the background fade, and I become almost laser-focused. It is my zone of genius. This is also a place of great peace, and it is where my best work comes from.

This zone of genius is where your no-bullshit self lives:

- The one that is not afraid to take risks

- The one that is not afraid to tell the truth

- The one that is not concerned with validation

- The one that creates for the simple, satisfying joy of creating

In this space, there is a creative rhythm that is almost musical, almost orgasmic. Because it is the destination we have been trying to reach all along. It is the perfect wave, the lover you long for, the song that makes your heart skip.

Your art can never be about the money - Danielle LaPorte

Traffic, bestselling books, speaking gigs, and all the accolades that your ego gets its rocks off on are just by-products of creating from places where your ego loses its power. It is counterintuitive.

The ego needs to be fed to remain healthy, but if you overfeed it, it vomits all over every part of your life. In addition, it is not the real YOU. When I have created something for attention, money or any form of external validation, that has been my ego at work. However, when I enter the space we are speaking of, my ego feels threatened and will do everything in its power to bring me back to playing the game on its level.

My ego has led to my most spectacular downfalls, and has led to the pursuit of things in life that mattered to it far more than they mattered to me. You might find that yours has led you similarly astray.

The "No bullshit" version of who you are can work with a compass. Your ego needs a map because it does not quite understand the wise words of Paul Jarvis, "Nobody is successful because they took somebody else's roadmap and copied it."

That should hang in high school gyms across America, and there should be fortune cookies at college graduations with that one message.

Imagine the beauty that would fill our world when we all stop wasting our unique gifts on the pursuit of becoming somebody else or the person we thought we should be.

What if we stopped suppressing the parts of ourselves

that take us through our most diverse range of emotions? Yes, you will be depressed sometimes. However, sometimes your brightest work will come from the darkest parts of your life.

When you hit rock bottom the only place to go is up. When I started reinventing myself, I literally saw my bank balance hit zero. My resume looked more like a rap sheet because of how many jobs I had had. For the first few weeks, I even got drunk in the middle of the day. I was in a really dark place. I questioned the purpose of my life and wondered whether I was put here to do anything that mattered. Some days I even thought, "the world would be better if I wasn't here. Maybe something bad will happen and I'll be gone soon."

But all of this was the spark for one of the most prolific and creative periods of my life. Since I hit rock bottom:

- I've started a blog that people actually read
- I've started my own show that people around the world listen to
- I've been a speaker at conferences
- I've written **The Small Army Strategy**, **The Extraordinary Achiever's Manifesto**, and some other things.
- I've become an avid surfer
- The brightest work emerged from one of the darkest parts of my life
- I had to recognize and explore the broken parts of who I am. However, in order to be the no-bullshit version of me, that was necessary.

- The small moments like coffee shop conversations with my oldest friends have been my greatest treasures

Books, destinations, and callings tend to reveal themselves to you while you pursue them. We often do not know where stories end, where unpaved roads lead, and who we'll become along the way. Therefore, you just have to start. As Justine Musk says, you will recognize the destination when you get there.

Your ego is the bullshit version of who you are, and ego-based creation is not your art.

YOU WON'T FIND A CALLING IN EGO-BASED LEARNING

"To get at the truth of your calling, you have to crack open that false self and see what lies within". ~ Justine Musk

What would you choose to learn if the only reward

was a sense of self-fulfillment?

Digging into the depths of your soul to find the REAL

you is something that many people avoid because

they are terrified of what they might find. In those

depths are our dark parts, imperfections, flaws, and

inadequacies.

However, that is also where the things that makes me

unmistakable and unforgettable lie.

- The part of me that is capable of making dents
  in the universe

- It's the part of me that is capable of pursuing a wild-eyed dream
- The part of me that can create art for the sake of art.
- It's the part of me that can experience the purest form of joy

However, this kind of self-exploration is not encouraged by society. There's no system designed for it. The closest thing to it is a mid-life crisis followed by years of therapy. That is, if you are lucky. Otherwise, you go to the grave with your music still in you, wondering about all the things you wish you had done.

I had a conversation a few months ago with a kid who quit going to school when he was roughly 12 years old. The most interesting thing he said to me when I asked him about designing his curriculum is that he never chose any of the things he wanted to learn based on their external value. Yet, for most of us, almost everything we choose to learn is based on the external value it might give us.

I took a semester of Japanese in college because in the movies people who could speak Japanese had corner offices, had dinner with hot girls, and wore nice suits. I've never had a corner office, I've only had dinner with a few hot girls, and the suit I wear most is a wet suit.

I took a semester of computer science at Berkeley because computer science graduates were in hot demand and it was the dot com boom. They got to this concept called recursion, my head almost exploded, and I dropped the class before I got an F.

The only reason I took those is that my first attempt at majoring in something for its external value, getting into the undergrad business program, was a failure.

I see it in the online world too. People want to learn how to do something not because of the joy it might bring to their lives, but because of the external accolades: traffic, book deals, and more clients. We all have things we could be learning and maybe if we did we could become the most interesting person in the world. (However, do not do it for that label). When I start most of my projects, it is because of the sense of fulfillment they bring to me.

Nobody had ever said to me, "Why not just study something you're interested in?" In my life, I have met very few people who actually use their college degrees. Engineers and computer scientists are maybe the only ones. The rest end up going to law school (I am kidding…kind of). I heard a story that on the first day of law school, professors ask, "How many of you are here because you don't know what else to do with your life?" Apparently, most people raise their hands.

My friend Shannon told me her daughter was going to college, and she asked me if I would advise my 18 year-old self not to go. My answer surprised me. I wouldn't tell my 18 year-old self to skip college. It had an impact on my life. At the time, we didn't have the world we do at our disposal. I had two pieces of advice, "Be open and study abroad."

- No five-year plan
- No straight and narrow path

With rare exception, a calling comes to you at a young age. My sister found hers at a very young age. I can see it in her eyes when she talks about the work she does. I can hear it in her voice. It is clear this is a calling, not a job.

For the rest of us, just be open to possibilities, and what might come from being an explorer of the world instead of trying to be a [pre-insert career aspiration of your choice]. Consider whether it is even your choice, or is it one that was a by-product of your social programming?

So what do you choose to learn? Something that you would enjoy doing; Even if you were not good at it.

I have always been a writer, but not a great one. I started writing when I was in high school. After I graduated from college, I wrote a 63-page autobiography, in 8 days.

I wrote a 40-page story about my first startup. It was some of my best work. I had nowhere to share it, so I emailed it to a few friends. 10 years later, that story has come full circle.

Probably the worst writing I ever did was my admission essays for business school. I hired an admission consultant and paid him $5000.00. I might as well have titled the essays "The Bullshit Version of Who I Am."

I do not even know why I wrote in the early days. There were no blogs then. There was nobody to read my work. However, I did it anyways. Therefore, that returns us to one simple point.

What would you choose to learn if there were no external rewards? What would you choose to learn if the only reward was a sense of self-fulfillment? That is where the ego disappears, art is created, and callings are found.

THE OTHER 20%

"Sometimes rainbows and unicorns do shoot out of your ass when you sit down to write" ~ Paul Jarvis

Somebody emailed me and said, "I can't write." I replied back and said, "Neither can I. 80% of my work is terrible. You read the 20% that I risk sharing."

Perfection in any sort of art is a fool's errand. What makes it art is that it is imperfect, and the beauty of it lies in the eyes of the beholder.

· Maybe you can write.

· Maybe we can all write.

· Maybe you can draw

· Maybe we can all draw

- Maybe you can sing

- Maybe we can all sing

Moreover, who is the authority on whether you do any of those things well? People will love your art and people will hate it. For example:

- I like movies that many people hate.
- I have the pop culture taste of a teenage girl (90210, OC, Hart of Dixie)

We may not have natural talent for everything. However, we could learn just about anything and get decent at it. According to Josh Kauffman, we can become competent at anything in 20 hours. Most people are not good at things when they start. However, to let this be an excuse for not starting kills the possibility of finding your zone of genius.

False starts are certainly better than standing still. Eventually, you have to be willing to suck at something long enough to get good at it. I see this with people who want to learn how to surf. They show up once or twice in 3 months and then write it off as a lack of talent. Surfing is amazing. Learning how to surf sucks. However, if you can get past the part where you suck - the 80% - you will get to experience the thrill of the part that is amazing, the 20%.

Take something from inception to launch. Make what Peter Sims calls little bets. The final product might be terrible. However, in it you will find the 20% that might lead to something much bigger and better. The most valuable thing that could come from shipping a failure is what you will learn from it.

Therefore, that is competence; what about mastery? Take inventory of your skills, your experiences, and the things that light your eyes up. 80% of your life will not be worthy of mastery, and that's fine.

- I don't want to become a master web designer
- I don't want to become a master chef (well maybe)
- I don't want to become a master programmer

To find that 20% of your life you consider worthy of mastery, figure out the 80% that is not. That usually lies within the things you would not do if somebody paid you a million dollars. If there is nothing you would not do for a million dollars, I do not know what to tell you. Set aside some of it for your future therapist.

"In the Zone of Genius, your ego is unnecessary; living there is its own reward. In the Zone of Genius, you cease to care about recognition or ostracism. Once you make a commitment to inhabiting your full potential, your ego is suddenly faced with extinction. It has been making excuses for you throughout your life. Now, if your commitment to taking your Big Leap is sincere, your ego will need to be shown the door. Unless you are lucky, your ego will probably not go quietly. It has a lifetime of employment history behind it" ~ Gay Hendricks, The Big Leap

Worrying about what other people think is a jail of our own creation, and the irony of it is those people are in the same jail with us

By many measures, I am not a success:

- Bank balance

- Fans/Followers (aka internet vanity metrics)

- GPA

The list that is all based on what my ego wants goes

on and on. In fact, I think that measuring my life by its standards is why my ego has such a prolific employment history. Chances are yours does too.

Sometimes, I think we make a decision to come up with our own definition of success, but we still let somebody else's definitions dictate how we measure that success.

However, should we even measure? In addition, if we do, how often?

"I've never once met a successful blogger who questioned the personal value of what she did." Seth Godin

Is constantly measuring how close we are to a goal

actually keeping us from getting there? A friend told me the other day, "Very few things are worth measuring on a daily basis." Yet metrics and measurements of all sorts dictate our lives on a daily basis. Do we just end up creating a different version of the hell we were trying to escape?

If you planted a tree, would it make any sense to keep digging up the roots to make sure it was growing?

You water it and have a bit of faith that it will grow.

For most of my career, I have been in a zone of absolute boredom, and I could not figure out why. Something became apparent the other day when I talked to my friend Ralph Quintero. I have a deep need to make things with my own two hands and see what I have made. That goes as far back as my kindergarten report card.

It said something along the lines of , "He enjoys playing with blocks, but he's kind of anti-social." They got one half right.

That need, what Dyana Valentine would a call a "super condition for greatness," was never met in the early part of my adult life. All I ever made was cold calls, and the only thing I saw were people who were pissed off that was I calling them. Actually, it was even worse because I could not see them. I had to imagine that for myself while sitting at a desk. However, by my ego's measure of success, I was crossing off the boxes and making progress.

In addition, sometimes with our creative pursuits, creation is its own reward. Others often look upon the idea of working on anything without some sort of guarantee of external reward with skepticism.

- How do you know it will work? -- I do not. I have absolutely no idea, and that is the point.

- What if it doesn't make any money or the amount you had doing it? -- At least I had fun doing it and I'll have something to show for my work (which is more than I can say for those damn cold calls)

- What if everybody hates it? -- Everybody will not. However, some people definitely will. I am not trying to create the next Honey Boo Boo. (Anybody with taste probably hates that).

- What if it never pans out? -- I will not die. I will not go to jail, and I probably will not go completely broke.

Well, let us consider this. How much time do you spend thinking about what other people think about you? It is probably more than you want to admit. So really most people are not spending that time on their opinions of me because they are too busy worrying about what other people think of them.

Worrying about what other people think is a jail of our own creation, and the irony of it is those people are in the same jail with us.

You may have to read that again.

Many people will never even start a creative endeavor. Moreover, if they start, they may not continue with a creative endeavor, because our traditional rewards system has conditioned them to expect an immediate gain of some sort. Art that provides its creator with an external reward long after the average person would quit is admired, but it is rarely encouraged.

YOU CAN BE BETTER OR DIFFERENT

Most of our lives have been driven by comparison. We've been ranked, categorized, and criticized from the time we were 5 years old. We're labeled as smart kids, dumb kids, creative kids, and non-creative kids, locking us into prisons we can't smell, taste or touch. So we compete within a system, based on rules, constantly trying to outdo the competition. Better grades, more prestigious schools, more impressive job titles, and bigger bank accounts drive us forward like sheep until we're about to fall off the edge of a cliff. The desire to keep up, be better, and outdo the competition has lulled us into submission and conformity.

A system is only capable of producing what its rules dictate. We repeat history, in hopes of rewriting a better version. But when you abandon the system, you create something that doesn't exist. You write history from scratch. You claim your birthright to change the world in some meaningful way, to make a dent in the universe.

Yes, I believe that it is every person's birthright to make a dent in the universe. Most people just don't claim it. Others search but can't find it. Those who do find it realize one thing. You won't find it by trying to be better. You only find it by being different.

That's how you reach an unmistakable path. It's the

most counterintuitive thing in the world because you'll be ridiculed and questioned, until a crowd gathers or as AJ Leon would say, you've stopped traffic. And when the crowd does gather they'll drown out the voices of the critics, dream crushers and naysayers.

The system is not designed to encourage this kind behavior, but it's only through a bit of intentional chaos we end up letting our imagination guide us to the places we might have never arrived.

You don't get there by following somebody else.

You don't get there by following instructions.

You get there by writing your own.

You get there by using a compass instead of a map.

You get there by taking an unpaved road, the scenic route.

You get there by taking one turn in a DIFFERENT direction.

THE RISK OF UNMISTAKABLE WORK

Artists, musicians, writers and creators of any sort that stand out in the world today must be unmistakable. It is the only option. You cannot just reach a bigger audience. If you keep watering down your work to cater to the masses, eventually you will be washed away. That will not help. You must let your soulprint mark your art. Explore the depths of your soul, the light parts, the dark parts, and even the questionable ones. Cross lines, personal and professional. That is the only way you'll know where they are. It might be career suicide, or the only thing that saves your career in a world where the rewards for standing out outweigh the ones for fitting in. You must put the no-bullshit version of you into how you show up in the world. It must permeate every cell in your body. It stops being something you do and it becomes who you are.

- This isn't safe.

- It's easier said than done.

- It will make you uncomfortable

- You will have to raise your hand, insist and volunteer

- You'll have to be open to the possibility that you're holding back

- You'll need to be aware of where you're hesitating

- You'll have to use your microphone to share your truth

- You'll have to be willing to walk along unpaved roads

- It has its risks, but also its rewards.

People spot it from a mile away. They hate it or they

love it. They call you a disservice to humanity or a "modern day Plato." I have been called both.

Either label is not as relevant as you might think since you are the final authority on EVERYTHING in your life.

In the words of John Mayer, "It's better to say too much than never to say what you need to say."

My friend Heather and I were talking about honesty in writing. She said, "It's like you're starting a no bullshit movement."

I think James Altucher actually started that movement. I just joined it because I found it so refreshing. It is exhausting to keep a facade of farting rainbows and sunshine when life has not gone according to plan.

There comes a point at which you have nothing left to lose. You have already experienced many of the so-called "failures" that life might throw at you. You become free to be what James would call a fearless blogger. Kamal Ravikant would call it sharing your truth.

You are free to say whatever you want and all the "negative" consequences of this kind of risk have already happened. The only way to really stand out online is to be honest.

What is the worst that could happen?

Here's my list:

1. Ex-Communicated from Corporate America and Deemed a Lousy Employee:

This ship sailed a few years ago. There is nothing left for me to lose here. Some people suck at being employees. I certainly did. That does not mean they don't and can't create value. I've created far more value for people outside of my corporate cage than I ever did as an employee.

When a person like Patrick Vlaksovkits writes a New York Times Best Seller and tells me, "I'm professionally unemployable by corporate America," I realize that maybe this is not such a bad thing. Business schools that would never accept him as a student use his books in their classes. I would be prouder of that than getting into the business school. One of my goals in life is to speak at NYU Stern, my dream business school that rejected me. Ideally, I would like to speak at their commencement. Ego never completely disappears and some of these are on the list to feed that maniac.

I have these 3 "just because they are ridiculous" goals:

1) Find myself in a position where I have to hire an anti-trust lawyer. The only people that hire anti-trust lawyers are people who have made some serious dents in the universe.

2) Speak at college graduation

3) Buy a sports team (I do not even watch sports). Laura Belgray said once that she would brag about the fact the she had dinner with me one day when I own a hockey team. I will try to see what I can do, and I'll be sure to invite her to the

owner's box if it happens.

Come up with some "just because they're ridiculous" goals.

2. No Job Security

The only secure jobs I know of are these: doctors and tenured professors. I have both in my family.

Having a job does not mean you have security. Not having a job does not mean you don't have security. As an entrepreneur, I can keep working as long as I can keep coming up with ideas.

We are going to be working much longer than many of us thought we would. Retirement never appealed to me anyway. Jon Stewart said that when the Pope retired he was going to read books and pray.

Sitting on my ass doing nothing sounds boring, so I think I will keep working until I am not physically capable of it. Zig Ziglar said people have achieved some remarkable things in their older years. My only notable achievements have been in my 30's.

3. Bad Credit

Many people work at jobs they hate just so they can pay debt. I think Dale Stephens made a wise observation: "Is defaulting or paying less really worse than working at a job you hate?" At some point, you can either decide you let the circumstances dictate your life or facilitate your life. It is all just a bunch of numbers, in boxes and on computer screens that fluctuate. I am sure some finance person just cringed.

4. Disappointing Other People

I am sure I have disappointed many people and not lived up to their expectations. But it's much easier to be a spectator sitting in the stands than it is to be an artist, athlete, or creator who is actually in the game, taking chances, being vulnerable, and looking foolish in order to get the things they want out of life.

5. 35 and Single

I guess I am stubborn. Being a person who spends his life stuck with somebody out of obligation as opposed to true love is something I just cannot get behind, even if it means I do it before the "expiration date"

that supposedly is on my head.

 So, what good can come out of it?

1. Smart People Call Me for Advice (sometimes)

I have a friend who kicked ass at Berkeley, went to

MIT for Business School, and worked for

McKinsey. She is damn smart and probably knows

people who are smarter than me. She called me for

advice on her startup, and I had to ask her why me. I

guess I have some useful advice for people who are

building startups. I told her what I thought, and I did

the only thing I could think of. I introduced her to

somebody in my network. Oh yeah, she is working

on a cool startup that is crowd funding medical

treatments in developing countries.

2. Returning to the First Wave

I think about leaving a note on my desk saying, "I had go to check on the waves," and buying a one-way ticket to Brazil to return to my very first wave. I'd like to see if the old guy who rented me my board the day I caught my first wave is still there.

3. Abandoning The Myth of Having It All Figured Out

Nobody has it all figured out. People are generally confused. Besides, if you woke up one morning, had it all figured out and there was nothing left to learn, you would be bored out of your mind. There will

always be things to figure out, problems to solve, and
unpaved roads to explore.

I THINK CHRIS BROGAN'S FRIDGE IS BROKEN

You probably read that title and said, "What the hell?" However, it is true. If you listen to my recent interview with Chris, he tells me about his broken fridge, which brings me to the point of today's post.

When we see somebody who is successful we tend to mimic instead of model.

We copy instead of innovate. I saw a TED speech by Brandon Stanton, who runs Humans of New York, and I wondered if somebody had created "Humans of LA." However, the gas costs for doing that would be astronomical and that would not be very original.

- We become pale imitations of our mentors/role

models at best and end up in the echo chamber at worst

- We worship heroes instead of becoming our own superheroes (something that Chris actually encourages).

When our lives are so publicly on display, it is very easy to look around you and think you want to trade lives with somebody. It is easy to think you want to be somebody else because they seem to have it all. However, what is the point in that? How will that make you unmistakable?

In a world where everybody has a voice, the only "personal brand" that will stand out is one that is honest, imperfect, vulnerable, and rough around the edges. When you polish anything too much, it loses the thing that makes it shine from within. Then we cannot trust it anymore.

I jokingly said I have been slowly committing career suicide with each of these essays. Then you have to consider another idea. If somebody does not like you for who you REALLY are, would you want to work for him or her anyway? In addition, given that we have entered an era in which you can choose yourself, how much does it really matter?

- I was an impostor for over a decade, pretending that I actually gave a damn about the work I did.

- I always told EVERYBODY what I thought they wanted to hear.

- I held back and rarely said what I was actually thinking.

- I tried to pretend that I was perfect, unafraid, and never let my guard down.

- The truth of who I was, the ultimate corporate misfit, scared me.

Keeping up that act was soul crushing.

You reach a point where the truth is all you have left to work with. There's nobody left to disappoint and nothing left to lose. Ships sail, lovers leave, licenses expire, and you are left with two choices. Stand and watch from the shore or get in the water and search for the perfect wave (the one that makes every moment of your existence worth it). Therefore, you start to make your truth your mantra, your soul print and the place you live from.

Sometimes you have to cross a line to know where it is and push other people out of their comfort zones. Moreover, once that line is crossed you will find it difficult to go back. It is a bit like being unplugged from the matrix.

People are afraid to cross the line over to complete honesty and imperfection because they worry about losing things they do not have or even worse, things they have but that do not REALLY matter to them. Keeping up an act of any sort is easier in the short term, but becomes soul draining as life goes on.

People do not attempt to create any art because they might not get the validation they had hoped for. The irony of it is that when you do not create anything for validation, you probably will get plenty of it. Moreover, if you create for the joy of creating, no matter how the world responds, at least you had fun doing it.

Be honest. Be Imperfect. Embrace Your Inner Misfit.

DON'T CHOOSE YOURSELF SO THE
GATEKEEPERS CAN CHOOSE YOU

It is true that gatekeepers are dying. The opportunity
to choose you, do something that matters, make dents
in the universe and leave your soul print in the sand is
more accessible than at any time in the history of
western Civilization.

- We hear the story of a person who tweets
  about things his dad says and gets a TV show.
- We hear the story of how Amanda Hocking
  self-published her book, sold over a million
  books and then ended up with a book deal.

Our world is filled with stories of people who chose
themselves first and were chosen by the gatekeepers

second. So we think, "Sure, I'll choose myself," while secretly hoping that a gatekeeper will choose us.

- Maybe somebody will notice that blog you are writing that nobody seems to be reading
- Maybe a Hollywood producer will stumble upon the film you have made and pull you into the limelight
- Maybe you will become the next viral sensation on iTunes or YouTube
- Maybe you will go from utter obscurity to fame, fortune and everything else you think you want

However, when you choose yourself so the gatekeeper will choose you, you forget that creation is its own reward. The people who chose themselves did not do it because the gatekeepers would eventually sing a different tune. They chose themselves because they wanted to create and share their work with the world. They wanted somebody's life to be touched by what they had done. All they truly cared about was building their own little corner of the world.

Start there. The accolades, awards, recognition and validation may never come. In addition, ironically, when you finally stop giving a shit about them, they seem to come in abundance. Even when you look at somebody who is slightly more successful, more famous, or has more traffic, you put him or her on a pedestal and turn him or her into a gatekeeper.

Be your own gatekeeper, tastemaker, and connoisseur of what matters. Do not choose yourself so the gatekeepers will choose you.

ART, INTEGRITY, AND METRICS

"The society that we were told would be here waiting for us is completely gone and is never coming back. You can either take the blue pill (become depressed about an artificial reality that is never going to return) or take the red pill." (Fully enter the Choose Yourself era and take advantage of its opportunities)
~James Altucher

Most of the technology tools at our disposal are nothing more than a box of crayons. They give us an opportunity for self-expression.

- You are free to color outside the lines.

- You can use as many or as few colors as you want.

You can make anything you want. I would recommend doing what you can do that nobody else could in the way you could do it. I have no idea what that it is. Just do something; you will figure it out.

You will get data points. You can keep adjusting until you have reached a point of no return.

Occasionally, you will have an opportunity to compromise on the integrity of your art in exchange for external accolades like money and metrics. Gatekeepers like publishers, producers, and advertisers will actually encourage this so you may be chosen.

- Honey Boo Boo was chosen.
- Snooky wrote a New York Times Best Seller.

Gatekeepers will make you compromise the integrity of your art and water down your work because they are only interested in exploiting your art for profit. They want you to reach the masses. They will throw you a bone if you do well. However, if your art gets destroyed in the process, they do not give a damn. A bestselling author (you probably read his blog) told me that if you do not sell 1000 copies in the first week you would never hear from them again…. Therefore, now you are stuck with art that you hate and somebody else who owns it. I have probably just lost any shot at a book deal by telling you that.

If you cross this line, you have entered dangerous territory.

We are about to enter an era in which the media is going to become completely fragmented. The convergence of the mainstream media and independently produced media is around the corner. So the pursuit of fame on the level that the gatekeepers encourage is a fool's errand designed to keep the people at top where they are (getting rich by producing shit that doesn't matter) and the people who make dents in the universe from popping red pills and disrupting the world with their art.

When I select guests for my show I can look at how famous somebody is, or whether they have a story worth sharing. Maybe the famous person will cause us to reach more people, get more downloads, and increase our traffic. Nevertheless, to interview them just because they are famous compromises the integrity of the art. I used to do that in the early days of what I was doing. Sure, we have had plenty of "famous" people, but finding them is easy.

115

- I consider the way I choose my guests a big part of my art.

- That is how we find the Greg Hartle's of the world.

- That is how we talk about no bullshit blogging with people like Megan Morris

- That is actually the most difficult part. Finding more people like them is what keeps me up at night (in a good way).

Do not compromise the integrity of your art for the metrics that will temporarily inflate your ego.

YOU'LL NEVER BE UNMISTAKABLE IF

- You try to copy and mimic your heroes and role models

- You're never open to the possibility that you're holding yourself back

- You're fearful of what other people will think of your bold ideas

- You're afraid to cross the line in order to discover where it is

- You have an intention of becoming "internet famous"

- You're afraid to try things that might not work (most of what you know how to do know was something that might not have worked)

- You seek validation in the art you create

- You choose every opportunity based on

117

money

- You've never considered why you do the work you do

- You get caught up in the ego-driven pursuit of a life that looks good on paper

- You ignore your misfit tendencies

You already know most of what you need to know. In addition, if you do not, you will discover it within yourself. Moreover, when you create from that place, there is no competition. Nobody can compete with the "No bullshit" version of who you are.

YOU ARE THE FINAL AUTHORITY ON YOUR LIFE

"It is important to begin with a willingness to feel good inside, because there's no sense enhancing other parts of your life at the expense of your inner well-being." –Clayton Christensen

In many ways, surfing has been about my inner well-being. The exercise, cool wardrobes, and all the other things are just fringe benefits to me. They are positive externalities of an activity that has no real economic value, but an intrinsic one that cannot even be measured.

When I talked to Dan Martell once, he asked me a question. "Are your goals worthy of your life?" I do not know how many people even stop to ask themselves that question, and it's one of the most important ones we could ask ourselves. Blinded by our own ambition, caught up in the ego-driven pursuit of a life that looks good on paper, we race towards our goals at he expense of our inner well-being. When I was 20, I dreamt of commission checks, Presidents Club, free trips and all the things that I thought came with a lucrative sales career. Instead, what I got was stomachaches, IBS, and some of the darkest days of my life. The goal was not worthy of my life, and some days it felt like it was going to cost me my life.

You are the final authority on your life. You are the CEO. In addition, according to my friend Megan, when you realize that failure does not really matter. The funny thing is almost nothing matters as much as you think it does when you realize you are the final authority. So much of what we think matters is based on the opinions of other people:

Does the publisher think your book is worth publishing?

My friend Torre could not find an agent who wanted to work with her, so after 6 months she self-published. A Hollywood producer tracked her down and bought the movie rights to her book. Instead of waiting to be picked, she got to pick the agent of her choice, and let the publishers bid for her book.

- Is your writing good enough to appear on a

major blog?

- Are you good enough to be on the basketball team?

- Did you score high enough to get admitted?

- Are you hot enough for that girl or guy to date you?

- Is anybody reading what you write? Usually in the first 6 months, it's just your mom.

- Have you done something that warrants an appearance on BlogcastFM?

I always get a laugh when people tell me this is their dream. They forget that I am just a beach bum that likes making things, and I am a person who has never been picked.

Have you received the popular kid's blessing?

In addition, does it really matter, because the following:

- According to AJ Leon, Remarkable Misfits will make their ruckus and make dents in the universe
- Instigators will cause us to think, question our purpose, and examine our lives.
- Erika Lyremark and Justine Musk will provoke us with a purpose
- Ordinary people do extraordinary things every single day

You are the final authority on it all. Your sign-off is the one that matters above all. You get to say whether you live a life filled with meaning and purpose. In addition, what that means to you is not going to be found on a map, but by using a compass. I do not know what the destination will look like when you get there. So just START. The view should be fantastic when you arrive. There is often scenic beauty at the end of an unpaved road.

LEAVE YOUR HEART ON THE STAGE

"No instruction, no road map, except perhaps a few vague comments about "seeing" the negative spaces surrounding the pile of objects. So you gave it a valiant effort, you drew your heart out, and despite the art teacher's wonderful supportive encouraging comments, "Great effort, Good job. We'll do this one hundred more times and you'll nail it" you" you saw the result from your effort glaring at you from the paper: It looked like a pile of scribbles" - Mark Kistler

Yesterday I got an email from AJ Leon because I needed something to update my speaker profile, and he said I left my heart on stage. And I started to wonder what would happen if we left our heart on stage every time we created anything.

All of our art, writing, music, painting, and more is a performance. But it's not the bullshit facade kind of performance that you put on during a job interview, when you're trying to impress some girl because you're afraid she won't like you, or when you're trying to convince somebody of something you're not. That's exhausting and there's no heart in it at all.

It's a bust your ass to shine, honest to a fault, no bullshit, zero apology performance. If you look at the work of some of the most successful people in the world you'll see it as the undertone. It isn't just something they do, it's who they are. It's the kind of performance where your heart and soul bleed. It leaves you exhausted, but smiling with tears of joy. It's not something that can be sustained, but it also doesn't need to be. The minute you try to sustain it, it turns into the first type of performance.

For this kind of performance, you have to immerse yourself so deep in your art and become so present that you can't possibly judge your creations. That's where the purest work is born. If you judge, doubt or question it, the art gets tainted.

Recently, I started this project of learning how to draw. Tennis balls and apples don't exactly make for work to be hung up in the Smithsonian. My dad saw the house that I drew and said, "This looks like a kindergartener drew it." Of course it does. But kindergarteners have no judgment about their art. The house gets drawn and you as a parent better damn well hang it on the refrigerator or suffer the wrath of an artist who takes that much pride in his or her creation.

This kind of performance comes from a place of flow where the process hijacks procedure in a way that lights your eyes up. The world around you fades and you become so absorbed in whatever you're doing that people call you absent-minded, accuse you of day dreaming, and write you off as a person with ADD. The irony, of course, is that something has your attention so deeply that everything else is just an interruption.

Dave Matthews seems to have this down. You go to a concert, and even if you're not a fan, it's mesmerizing to watch him. The combination of lights, music, and environment make for a hell of a show. Maybe the giant cloud of marijuana smoke that fills the air adds to it. He leaves a mark on the audience every single time. If you haven't been to a Dave Matthews Show, I recommend it. I'm not even the biggest fan, but in concert it's something you can't miss.

What's amazing is when we're kids we are discouraged so much from this kind of behavior that we spend our adult lives doing yoga, surfing, meditating, seeing therapists and doing damn near anything to get to this pure place of creativity.

Try this for a few days. Set up Moleskine or journaling software the night before. Make sure it's the first thing you see when you turn on the computer. It's a little productivity hack called activation energy that I read about in Sean Achor's book **The Happiness Advantage**.

Set a timer and for the next 30 minutes try to make a

dent in the universe.

It's such a vague instruction that some people will get fed up and return to checking email, updating Facebook, tweeting, etc, etc. (I do all of those things too). But the instruction is purposely vague because to make unmistakable dents that make our heart and soul bleed, the instructions can't be too specific. This is the opportunity to tattoo your soulprint across the hearts and minds of humanity.

It's the opportunity for a performance where you leave your heart on the stage.

Made in the USA
Lexington, KY
29 January 2014